A SHORT HISTORY OF MONSTERS

Miller Williams Poetry Series
EDITED BY BILLY COLLINS

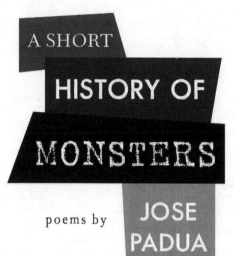

A SHORT

HISTORY OF

MONSTERS

poems by   JOSE
PADUA

The University of Arkansas Press
Fayetteville
2019

ISBN: 978-1-68226-094-4
eISBN: 978-1-61075-663-1

23 22 21 20 19   5 4 3 2 1

Designed by Liz Lester

♾ The paper used in this publication meets the minimum requirements
of the American National Standard for Permanence of Paper
for Printed Library Materials Z39.48-1984.
Library of Congress Cataloging-in-Publication Data

Names: Padua, Jose, 1957–   author.
Title: A short history of monsters / poems by Jose Padua.
Description: Fayetteville : The University of Arkansas Press, 2019. |
Identifiers: LCCN 2018037836 (print) | LCCN 2018038881 (ebook) | ISBN
9781610756631 (electronic) | ISBN 9781682260944 (pbk. : alk. paper)
Classification: LCC PS3616.A33624 (ebook) |
LCC PS3616.A33624 A6 2019 (print) | DDC 811/.6—dc23
LC record available at https://lccn.loc.gov/2018037836

Funded in part by

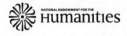 

To Heather Davis

CONTENTS

SERIES EDITOR'S PREFACE

When the University of Arkansas Press invited me to be the editor of its annual publication prize named in honor of Miller Williams—the longtime director of the press and its poetry program—I was quick to accept. Since 1988, when he published my first full-length book, *The Apple that Astonished Paris,* I have felt keenly indebted to Miller. Among the improvements to the world made by Miller before his death in January 2015 at the age of eighty-four was his dedication to publishing a poet's first book every year. He truly enjoyed finding a place for new poets on the literary stage. In 1990, this commitment became official when the first Arkansas Poetry Prize was awarded. Fittingly, upon his retirement, the prize was renamed the Miller Williams Poetry Prize.

When Miller first spotted my poetry, I was forty-six years old with only two chapbooks to my name. Not a pretty sight. Miller was the one who carried me across that critical line, where the "unpublished poets" impatiently wait, and who made me, in one stroke, a "published poet." Funny, you never hear "unpublished novelist." I suppose if you were a novelist who remained unpublished you would stop writing novels. Not the case with many poets, including me.

Miller Williams was more than my first editor. Over the years, he and I became friends, but even more importantly, before I knew him, I knew his poems. His straightforward, sometimes folksy, sometimes witty, and always trenchant poems were to me models of how poems might sound and how they could *go.* He was one of the poets who showed me that humor had a legitimate place in poetry—that a poem could be humorous without being silly or merely comical. He also showed me that a plain-spoken poem did not have to be imaginatively plain or short on surprises. He was one of my literary fathers.

Miller occupied a solid position on the American literary map, though considering his extensive career and steady poetic output, it's surprising that his poems don't enjoy even more prominence. As his daughter became the well-known singer and recording artist that she is today, Miller came to be known as the father of Lucinda Williams. Miller and Lucinda even appeared on stage together several times, performing a father-daughter act of song and poetry. In 1997, Miller came to the nation's attention when Bill Clinton chose him to be the inaugural poet at his second inauguration. The poem he wrote for that day, "Of History and Hope," is a meditation on how "we have memorized America." In turning to the children of our country, he broadens a nursery rhyme question by asking "How does *our* garden grow?" Miller knew that occasional poems, especially for occasions of such importance, are notoriously difficult—some would say impossible—to write with success. But he rose to that occasion and produced a winner. His confident reading of the poem before the nation added cultural and emotional weight to the morning's ceremony and lifted Miller Williams to a new level of popularity and respect.

Miller was pleased by public recognition. What poet is immune? At home one evening, spotting a headline in a newspaper that read POET BURNS TO BE HONORED, Miller's wife Jordan remarked "They sure have your number." Of course, it was the day dedicated annually to honoring Robert Burns.

Miller's true legacy lies in his teaching and his career as a poet, which covered four decades. In that time, he produced over a dozen books of his own poetry and literary theory. His poetic voice tends to be soft-spoken but can be humorous or bitingly mordant. The poems sound like speech running to a meter. And they show a courteous, engaging awareness of the presence of a reader. Miller knew that the idea behind a good poem is to make the reader feel something, rather than to merely display the poet's emotional state, which has a habit of boiling down to one of the many forms of misery. Miller also possessed the authority of experience to produce poems that were just plain wise.

With Miller's sensibility in mind, I set out to judge the first year's contest. I was on the lookout for poems that resembled Miller's. But the more I read, the more I realized that applying such narrow criteria would be selling Miller short and not being fair to the entrants. It would make more sense to select manuscripts that Miller would enjoy reading for their own merits, not for their similarity to his own poems. That his tastes in poetry were broader than the territory of his own verse can be seen in the variety of the books he published. The list included poets as different from one another as John Ciardi and Jimmy Carter. Broadening my own field of judgment brought happy results, and I'm confident that Miller would enthusiastically approve of this year's selections, as well as those in previous years.

This year, the work of two very different poets, who have readability, freshness of language, and seriousness of intent in common, stood out from the tall stack of submissions. Miller would be pleased to know that, as it turned out, this will be a first book for the both of the two winners, born thirty-five years apart.

In the process of judging *A Short History of Monsters* by Jose Padua, I read his poems, set them aside, then picked them up and again and so on. I kept setting them back down mostly because of their unruly shapes. Line lengths vary wildly as do stanza size and shape. They give the impression of being typed up without much of a plan. Adding to this informality is their tone. "Conversational" does not quite get it. If I were to review these poems in a workshop, I would have several big suggestions. I tend to follow Mary Oliver's suggestion that "our poems should at least be tidy." Yet the poems won me over by taking me on associative rides that ended at surprising destinations, thus providing one of the thrills of reading lyric poetry. Thereafter, I began to see that their haphazard looks perfectly fit the energetic talk that drives the poems.

Padua wastes no time in getting the reader inside a poem. With openings like "When I was a kid/ I thought that the greatest record ever made…" and "My friend Michael and I/ are sitting at an outdoor cafe/ on Avenue A/ drinking beer,/ when we spot Lady Miss Kier,/ the singer of the hot new band/ Deee-Lite," how can we do anything but hop on board? The quickness of his associations and his inventive images maintain our interest to the end. We are the happy riders on the stream of Padua's consciousness.

Padua is a man of his time. His poems do not take place in some cloudy sphere of lyricism. Instead, they react to the world around them. Headlines like the announcing the fall of Hanoi and the catastrophe of the Challenger space shuttle are part of this poet's sensorium. Such notable events act as markers of the poet's past. Like the rest of us, Padua also locates himself in time by what songs are playing on the radio—"I could almost feel Casey Kasem fighting back the tears." And his capacious poems have room for everyone. Grace Kelly, Dr. Seuss, Henry Miller, "the amazing Kreskin," and Marcus Welby are just a few of the figures who come into play here and who constitute a background of American history and culture against which the poet's stories are told.

For me, Padua's best abilities are showcased in "MacArthur Park," a poem about the song with the same title, which his younger self sees as "a flash of wisdom," a song so "sensual as to make Fanny Hill / seem like a Lyndon Johnson State of the Union Address in comparison." For Padua, the song not only evokes the climate of the late sixties, but makes him wonder about its meaning. After all, does not the song raise "some serious questions?" Who left the cake out in the rain? What was the meant by that "sweet green icing falling down?" This outbreak of English-major questions comes from a younger, more innocent Padua, for whom just about everything is fascinating. But this phase soon devolves into disillusionment and doubts, even about the afterlife. The last movement of the poem (it has its own musical progression) sees the poet dressed up in partly borrowed clothes for his mother's funeral. It's 1994. We have left the sixties behind, and now "MacArthur Park" is "a stupid song from the summer of love that no longer moved me, / [and] had nothing to do with either life or death." This poem and others made it clear that underpinning the loose associative riffs of Padua's talk are some of the ancient themes of poetry, and that beneath the mad surfaces of his poems, there was a smart, sympathetic mind at work.

One Padua poem contains the Bukowski-like claim that "the only talents I have / are for drinking beer / and fucking up." I think now we can safely enlarge that list to include his talent for writing lively, soulful poems.

Billy Collins

ACKNOWLEDGMENTS

Thanks to the editors and publishers of the following journals, anthologies, chapbooks, and websites where some of these poems first appeared in different form: *ACM* (*Another Chicago Magazine*): "On the Far Edge of the European Theater"; *Berkeley Poets Cooperative*: "Eve of Celebration Blues"; *Big Cigars*: "The Invention of Jack Kerouac," "Why I'm So Much Greater Than Everyone Else"; *Body Double*: "End of the Parade"; *Bomb*: "On These Days Driving"; *Café Review*: "Science Fiction"; *The Complete Failure of Everything* (chapbook), Apathy Press: "Avenue Banana," "Deep End," "I Can't Find My Money," "Power Lunch," "September Song," "The Sporting Life," "Strange Dreams"; *Downtown*: "Night of the Living Dead"; *Exquisite Corpse*: "The New York City Marathon," "On Broadway"; *Meow: Spoken Word from the Black Cat* (CD): "Pulp Fiction"; *Mondo Barbie*: "Barbie"; *The National Poetry Magazine of the Lower East Side*: "The Invention of Jack Kerouac"; *Rant*: "A True Star"; *Redtape*: "Darkness and Doubt," "A Short History of Everyone in the World"; *Salon.com*: "New York"; *Shaking Like a Mountain*: "Man on the Moon"; *Short Poems for the Long Road* (chapbook), P.O.N. Press: "81 St. Mark's Place," "My Own Like Poem"; *The St. Mark's Poetry Project Newsletter*: "The Complete Failure of Everything"; *Strange Dreams* (chapbook), P.O.N. Press: "Chivalry," "Pet Sounds," "Work"; *Tribes*: "About Strangers' Houses"; *Unbearables Portfolio One*: "The Big One"; *WordWrights*: "The Angel of 11th Street."

Thanks to Michael Simms, Carl Watson, Eddie Dean, Michael Randall, Lori Andiman, Tom DiVenti, Debbie Martin, Ed Hamilton, Jeffrey McDaniel, Silvana Straw, Kenneth Carroll, Joel Dias-Porter, Andy Fenwick, David Rattray, Maggie Estep, Bart Plantenga, Ron Kolm, and Richard Peabody for various forms and measures of inspiration and encouragement. Thanks to Molly Bess Rector for helping to clean up some loose ends in the manuscript while still allowing these ends to wander as is their wont; thanks to Billy Collins for taking the time to really *read* me.

Thanks to Cosme T. Padua, Margarita S. Padua, Anthony Padua, and Patricio Padua for being there; to Margarita Mei Padua and Julien Padua for motivation and for keeping me awake; and to Heather Davis for everything.

I.

Man on the Moon

Darkness and Doubt

Walking upstairs to my apartment one evening
I heard the little girl who lives next door,
on seeing me, whisper to her friends,
"Oh oh, here comes the monster."
I stopped outside my door, turned to them
and said, "Little boys and little girls,
everything is terror and anguish.
You'll grow up to lead lives
of heartbreak, misery, and desperation.
Everything you want will be in the hands of someone else.
Everything you need will be denied you,
and the only thing you'll ever see
is the darkness of your own mad fantasies."
They looked at me and started
laughing wildly, ecstatically.
I smiled back at them, then walked into my apartment
and shut the door.
They were a nice group, those boys and girls,
and smart too, because even
at such a young age,
they could handle my demons
a lot better than I could.

Avenue Banana

Living on Avenue Banana
in the 1990s is not a lot like
drinking tea. I look up to the sky.
You shout at people driving by
in limousines. We eat rice and
chicken, wonder what to do.
You could go home and watch
your color TV or whistle on the way
to the sink. I can lie back on my
mattress like a tiny buffalo
and wave my hands at the flies
in the air or on my knee. Alone,
I see white paint chips on the ceiling,
feel the need for something green or
golden. With you there's sometimes
a step in between, you sitting
in my window reading a magazine.
Sometimes we're watching
the same movie on different TVs.
Other times I'm giving you cigarettes
like moonlight by the sea. And
though this isn't Paris in the 1930s
and I can't be Henry Miller and you
can't be Anaïs Nin, the look in your
eyes sometimes makes me think
of you as Grace Kelly in bed reading
a copy of Vogue, and me as Jimmy
Stewart, asleep by the window
with two broken legs.

Pulp Fiction

This afternoon a bum on the street mistook me for a drug addict.
"It's that CRACK that's making you sweat," he advised.
I nodded and said, "Yeah, I really ought to quit"
as people walking near me picked up their pace to get away from me.

Later, I'm crossing the street when a carload of scraggly-haired kids
       pulls up beside me.
"Hey, man, you got any rolling papers?" one of them asks.
"No," I say, "I just drink, that's it."
"Come on," he says, "just give them to me, all you Filipino
       motherfuckers smoke reefer."
I keep quiet and walk ahead as they start to jeer and yell at me.

It's been said that the meek shall inherit the earth,
but I've got bruises on my arms from running into people
on the street who expect me to scurry out of their way like a rat.
I've got dark patches on my soul from people moving out of *my* way
because they think I'm going to kill them.

People either see me as the lamb who's ready to sacrifice himself
to the gods of their ambition
or as the wolf who's going to set his fangs upon them,
tear them limb from limb, eyeball from eyeball.
The truth is somewhere in between.

"Do you speak English?" people in bars ask me.
"No," I tell them, "I'm from France, I speak French."
"You're not from around here, are you?" other people say to me.

"No, I'm not," I answer. "I'm from Saturn and I'm here to mate with
        Earth women.
Is that your sister sitting next to you? Nice tits."

It's been said that he who makes a beast of himself diminishes
the pain of being a man.
So I drink straight from the bottle till hair grows on my cheeks.
I swipe the drinks from other drinkers
as fur forms on the back of my neck.

"I was born here," I used to say,
"I ate my first McDonald's cheeseburger when I was four,
recited the Pledge of Allegiance for teacher when I was six,
and by the age of seven I could speak the language better than
        you do now."

It's been said that the truth will set you free,
but whenever I speak the truth no one believes it,
and whenever I hear the truth it makes me feel like a prisoner
on death row.

So, I tell stories to keep the truth alive without telling it.
So I create truth to keep me from becoming history:

I was raised by flying cockroaches until the age of seventeen. Could
        you lend me a buck?
I'm a crack-head pimp from the planet Liechtenstein. Would you
        like a job?

I'm a millionaire from Muffberg, Ohio. I came here two years ago
       with a dollar in my pocket and a smile I could pry open
       doors with. Would you like a tip on the stock market?
I'm vice president of a mid-sized consulting firm making two hundred
       grand a year tax free. Can I pay for your groceries?
I'm Johnny Depp's garbage man, wanna go out?
I'm Conan O'Brien, wanna fuck?

This is the way I spend my days.
This is the way I earn my nights,
walking the earth telling lies, spreading rumors:

"And blessed is he who in the name of charity and good will
shepherds the weak and ignorant through the valley of darkness
for he is truly his brother's keeper.
But I will strike down upon thee with great vengeance
and furious rebukes those who attempt to poison and destroy
my brothers
and you will know my name is The Lord
when I lay my vengeance upon thee."

It's been said what doesn't kill you makes you stronger.
I think what doesn't kill you lets you live longer.
There's a difference.

About Strangers' Houses

From the outside
they look safe, warm,
and comfortable.

On the inside
there are horrible smells,
blood stains on the carpet,

and in the kitchen,
attached to the refrigerator
with a magnet shaped
like a slice of pie,

is a note that reads:
"Aunt Sally is in the attic.
She was too heavy to move."

New York

After Allen Ginsberg

I used to take long walks at dawn in New York,
staying up all night in my roach-infested fourth floor walk-up
on Avenue B, drinking cheap wine, baring my soul to
the bathroom mirror as I contemplated easy listening music,
having beatific visions of aggressive shoe salesmen
while the angelic rants of harried personnel managers,
brainstorming ad executives, and the insane followers of trends
echoed through the caverns of my vacant, unilluminated mind.

Dragging myself through the gentrified streets of the Lower East Side
                  of Manhattan
in search of a cheap breakfast special of scrambled eggs and sausage,
looking up to the sky waiting for Pussy Galore to parachute down from
the heavens like in *Goldfinger*, my head got dizzy,
not because of the magnitude of the heavens that floated
over the route of every Greyhound bus in America and every desolate
flower in the world, but because the blood was rushing away from
                  my brain.

Expelled from the academy for acting like an asshole,
my copy of *The Tibetan Book of the Dead* remained unread;
Jack Kerouac was just someone I read when I was in high school
because he seemed like a writer who knew how to party;
to me the name William Blake meant as much

as the name William Hurt, just another sensitive guy
you had to know really well in order to call him "Bill."

Whether I was dead broke or living on credit,
working a straight job marketing costume jewelry through the mail,
or writing stories off the top of my head
for alternative newspapers to make a few easy bucks,
I was always the con man without a clue,
the pool hustler who scratched on the eight ball,
the actor who didn't know how to tend bar or wait tables,
the musician who couldn't keep time or play in tune,
the poet who hated poetry and poets and pretty much everything
                else as well.

One of the second-best minds of my generation,
I was suffering in a second-rate way,
always desperate but never starving,
always angry but never mad.

Sometimes I worked and sometimes I didn't.
Sometimes I got jobs just waiting by the phone—
"I want two thousand words, on my desk, Monday morning.
                Serial killers."
Other times I lost jobs coming in on time
wide awake and smiling as the previous night's bourbon wafted
out of my pores like a can of air freshener that was packaged in hell.

New York, city of opportunity, where when my girlfriend
dumped me for the first time I went out and ended up with a twenty-three
year old model/actress who was Steve Buscemi's brother's roommate.
Man was I connected, if only I'd had an idea for a screenplay it
would have taken me at least another year before I went broke.
New York, I knew someone there who knew someone who knew
            Allen Ginsberg.
New York, I knew someone there who knew someone who thought
            he'd once been abducted by a UFO.

New York, where six degrees of separation are cut in half,
where the half-life of radium 226 triples like a human embryo
at a fertility clinic, and where a quart of bourbon
will get you one gallon drunk on any day of the week except Wednesday.

New York, where I was in a band called Lord Burlap,
playing sloppy guitar for a high-strung, bald-headed singer who stuttered
when he talked and was an all-around good guy and good friend of mine
until he decided that he wanted to kill me.

New York, where on a day after I appeared on national television
reading a poem, I wandered the streets feeling like I'd completely
            sold out
and gotten nothing in return.

New York, where I chatted up my connection for writing a soft-core
            porn novel

on the corner of 14th Street and 3rd Avenue as the mustard from the hot dog
I'd just gotten from a street vendor dripped to the ground.

New York, where one snowy winter day I watched the smoke rise from
out of the bowels of the World Trade Center
the first time they tried to blow it up.
I lay in front of my 12-inch
black and white TV set refusing to answer the phone,
believing that illumination, Buddha, Mohammed, Jesus, L. Ron Hubbard,
and Dr. Ruth were beyond me,
and hoping that for God's sake those people would quit calling me.

New York, where Allen Ginsberg got old and turned into one really
                    creepy, self-righteous
guy who couldn't go for two minutes without quoting Kerouac.

There's no time to be connected now,
no time to wander desolate under the starry dynamo of the
                    American night,
no time to follow gurus and scholars and aging hipsters.

Allen Ginsberg died in 1997.
Allen Ginsberg wrote a few good poems back in the fifties,
then starting chanting and taking his clothes off in public at every
                    opportunity

as he bade us to watch and listen.

Allen Ginsberg suffered for his art, then it was our turn.

I left New York in 1993.

I was younger then, but not that much younger.

I too suffered for my art. Now it's your turn.

Eve of Celebration Blues

Though the Disney kids
wear clothes from Sears,
I'll bet they never had to decide
where to bury

their dead goldfish.
Me, I got my first guitar
at Sears. It sounded tinny
and made noise like feedback,

which was strange, it being
an acoustic guitar. I got
my first goldfish there too,
and they made strange noises as well,
especially when I plugged them in.

Science Fiction

In the spring of 1968
we had the riots.
I remember the smoke rising in the sky,
the sound of sirens and our next-door neighbors

laughing as they came down the alley
carrying TVs, air conditioners, entire racks
of sport coats, dress shirts, evening gowns.
Later we saw the shells of burned-out buildings,

the broken streetlights and the National Guard
patrolling the streets, soldiers in charge
of a conquered land.
We stayed inside while our friends

played with their new toys
and their parents tried on their new clothes
or watched their new TVs
with the sound turned up loud.

Eventually things were the same as before—
the rich kids decked out in polka dots
and paisley in Georgetown, buying drugs,
playing guitars, chanting "Om" and "Hare Krishna"

as our neighbors' toys broke and the colors
on their new clothes faded.
By September we were back in school
and the girl next door got pregnant

and her brothers robbed stores,
mugged pedestrians, got thrown in jail.
And remembering the riots,
when the chaos on the streets

lent support to the vision in our minds,
those nights when, after the smoke had cleared
and the sirens had faded,
you'd look up to the sky

and see a thousand and one stars—
I can't help but feel nostalgic.
Like passengers on a raft in the days
when men believed the earth was flat,

we were explorers, riding bravely, peacefully,
to the end of the earth
and the next war
of the worlds.

MacArthur Park

When I was a kid I thought
the greatest record ever made
was the 1968 mod orchestral rendering
of Jimmy Webb's lost-love opus, "MacArthur Park."
For me, "MacArthur Park" was a flash of wisdom, an epiphany as great
as an apostle's brief glimpse of heaven,
and an experience so innately sensual as to make Fanny Hill
seem like a Lyndon Johnson State of the Union Address by comparison.
As sung by that great drunken actor, Richard Harris
(who, if they'd had videos in those days, would appear crooning the words
decked out in love beads, mirrored sunglasses, and a paisley
                Nehru jacket),
"MacArthur Park" was Fellini's *La Dolce Vita*, Beethoven's Fifth
                Symphony,
and Dr. Seuss's *Green Eggs and Ham*
all boiled down to five bittersweet minutes
in the American summer of love.
I'd always stop what I was doing to reflect,
to meditate like a pilgrim at the end of that long, tortuous journey
through the slough of despond whenever it came on the radio.
I could almost feel Casey Kasem fighting back the tears
every time he sent it out as a long-distance dedication.
I could almost see the women in their yellow satin dresses
swoon as the song, after traveling through the airwaves,
came out of the speakers like a succubus wearing Old Spice cologne.

For me "MacArthur Park" was no one-hit wonder or one-night stand,
no temporary truce or let-the-sun-shine-in, fly-by-night Broadway craze.
For me "MacArthur Park" was the fall of Hanoi, an ether binge,

an up-against-the-wall, motherfucker-are-you-part-of-the-solution-or-are-
    you-part-of-the-problem,
Evel Knevel motorcycle leap into the great beyond.
And, like all great works of art, "MacArthur Park" raised some serious
    questions.
For example, who was the miscreant who left that cake out in the rain?
And what exactly was that recipe that he'd never have again?
Yes, these metaphors were deep, giving me forlorn visions
of that "sweet green icing falling down" in the dark,
of drinking "the wine while it is warm" with no one
ever catching me "looking at the sun."
I often quoted them in love letters
I wrote to my first teenage crush,

believing they would make me out to be a profoundly sensitive
young man whose passions she'd be foolish to deny.
It was no wonder she sent the letters
back to me.

This, of course, was some years before The Silver Convention's
seminal "Fly, Robin, Fly" rid me of my more sentimental proclivities.
Before I sat back in cataleptic paralysis like one of Marcus Welby's
    patients
as a friend of mine from high school began singing
"They're Coming to America" along with Neil Diamond
when that hideous song came on the radio.
Before I cringed in late-night horror film terror while another friend
began chanting, "We got a great big convoy, running through the night,

we got a great big convoy, ain't she a beautiful sight?"
as we headed east on Route 50 toward the beach in the dead of winter.

It was about this time when I began having
doubts about the afterlife.

When I stopped believing in ESP, astral projection, pyramid power,
speed reading, streaking, and the amazing Kreskin.

When I stopped believing that the government was on my side.

When I stopped believing that the concept of America included me
whether I was rich or poor,

white or something else.

When I stopped having faith in God and the entire world.

It was all so long ago.

I was dressed in the blue wool suit I'd grown into since high school,
a stiff white shirt that reeked of too much starch, a red silk tie
I'd borrowed from my father, and the black
leather shoes my brother had bought me for the occasion.

It was 1994. It was cloudy and cold with gray sunlight flowing through
the stained-glass windows as a priest gave me instructions
on how to read a passage from the Bible.

It was the same priest who had mumbled his way through
the rosary during the wake the night before like a drunken Elvis impersonator
going through the motions of putting on a show,

the priest who would later put words into my dead mother's mouth—
a priest who had never met her, who had never known
of her existence until she was gone—

saying from the top of the pulpit with his head held high
in self-righteousness how if she were here with us today
she'd be asking us to take the time to consider
and reflect upon our lives as Christians.

Holy Christ, I thought, she'd never ask us to do that.
Because if she were alive and at a funeral she would have
shown some genuine respect for the dead,
turned her head toward the ground, allowing the dead to speak
      through silence.
And though I'd always shouted out from among the crowd at the fools
on stage, demanding from them some measure of truth,
I sat there in silence loosening my tie as he delivered a sermon, which,
like a stupid song from the summer of love that no longer moved me,
had nothing to do with either life or death.

My First Poem

If I remember correctly,
my first poem was written for
some girl I knew in my
high school days.
She had straight, shoulder-length hair,
pale pink skin, and spoke with
the slightest trace of a lisp.
She listened to The Captain and Tenille, Neil Sedaka,
and "Tie a Yellow Ribbon Round the Old Oak Tree"
while I read Samuel Beckett, listened
to Albert Ayler's "Spirits Rejoice," and
thought constantly about death.

Things aren't all that different nowadays.
Just looking across the street and seeing
a television through someone's window
makes me think of heart attacks and hospital beds.
The sight of flowers and trees and
U-Haul minivans reminds me of
cemeteries and tombstones.
And though at times I may seem to be some
strange bon vivant drunkard, half
man, half whiskey bottle,
I am really just another middle-aged
misfit, trying to think
of the ways I might save my life
into old age

and some semblance
of contentment.
But, like the girl for whom
I wrote my first poem,
the ways elude me,
and like the contrails
from behind a jet plane,
they vanish in the air.

It's an old story that's been told
too often and too loudly—
matter meeting antimatter
and the resultant destruction
of everything we hold sacred,

or else being in the same car
on the same road
for so many years
that the best thing left
is to drive off quietly into
the night,

but in the middle of the journey
through all these roadside attractions
and breakfast stops,
and through the rising and falling
of forests and mountains,

the greatest beauty is in
those spaces where we don't connect,
the moments of silence between cities—
the rest is comfort:
the way I start to shout
while you look away pretending not to know me,
the way you watch people at a bar
while I stare into my drink and laugh,
the way your eyes widen
and your voice rises
and your body shines,
the way you walk with the grace
and confidence
over which countries are divided
and men prepare
for a hundred
years of war.

Man on the Moon

The radio is tuned to some oldies station
when a siren begins to wail outside, spinning lights
around the walls like lazy butterflies tethered by
the diminished gravity of the moon.

I was ten or twelve or maybe eight,
watching television in the living room
with my mom and dad, leaning up against
the coffee table or else sitting back
against the old blue sofa with ice cream stains,
believing, when they put a man on the moon,
that all things were possible.

I used to pray, "Oh Lord, don't let them drop that
bomb, don't let them send me to fight, and
please make that girl with the
ponytail and braces mine."
I can't remember her name now—
she lived down the street—
and sitting next to my mother's hospital bed
on the last night of her life,
I couldn't remember what it was
I ever feared about the bomb.

II.

American Dream

Barbie

I am Barbie.
I live in your dollhouse.
You change my clothes every day.

If I could get out
of here I would
kill you all.

The Invention of Jack Kerouac

In a bookstore today,
in the section on UFO abductions,
I began to see stars
and strange planets,
vast dark spaces
and bug-eyed humanoids
traveling faster than the speed of light..
I was so moved I slipped a book
into my inside coat pocket.

I picked up a book about
the Hells Angels and
heard the roar of motorcycles
had visions of sexy women
with beer bellies
who cursed a lot
and ate thick hamburgers.
I went to the cashier
with this book
and paid for it.

I decided to steal
the UFO book and pay
for the one on the Hells Angels
because bikers scare me more
than aliens from outer space do.
It's that and

the influence of the wheel.

If the wheel were never invented

we wouldn't have motorcycles.

And if the wheel had never been turned

over on its side

we wouldn't have flying saucers.

We'd have no truck stops,

no highways,

no Jack Kerouac to write *On the Road*,

just men and women

on horseback

and sailing ships

under a sky filled

with what might be stars

and the sparks

of roman candles.

Strange Dreams

I felt bad.

I was wearing brightly colored clothes and tight shoes.

I had a haircut that made people with bad haircuts laugh at me.

I had underwear that was dirty and stuck out above my pants.

I was born in this country but didn't look like I could speak the language.

I was born without the usual weapons: looks, personality, a chainsaw.

I bought things that were not cheap, but cheap-looking.

I had an annoying rectal itch.

I felt like I was tripping but everything was in black and white and
    looked pretty much the same.

I had the irritating habit of calling everyone Buddy.

I was cursed at by Hare Krishnas.

I was spat upon by nuns.

I had never eaten brunch until I was well into my thirties.

I was twelve years old when I first saw a potato chip.

I was fifteen years old when I had my first bowel movement.

I used to laugh at people who ate pizza with anchovies, but not anymore.

I used to go to the theater to View Films but now I Watch Movies.

I used to read poetry and novels but now I read *The Weekly World News*.

I used to eat free range poultry but now I eat Spam.

I used to eat tofu and sprouts but now I *am* Spam.

I once knew how to get things started at parties.

I was once a member of the Communist Party but then I discovered
    stamp collecting.

I once had a normal life but then I became a poet.

I was once a poet but then I became a performer.

I was once a performer but then I became a dried apricot.

I used to say a lot of things in a cute way but now I usually lie uneaten

in a bowl on someone's cocktail table in New Jersey when
company is around.
I have a feeling in my bones that someone great is watching over me.
I just hope he doesn't see when I slip the cough syrup into my pocket.

And there were roses in the spring
and cherry blossoms and magnolias along the Avenue
and people were dressed in the finest linen and lace
and the air had the taste of honeysuckle
and the dogs ran free where the marble sidewalks ended.

I was dreaming strange dreams of Paris,
of Chinese dumplings and Turkish coffee,

of being wanted for murder and everyone knowing my face,
and I was dreaming I was a monkey at the zoo,
swinging on a tiny trapeze, howling at the oddity
of the human faces that watched me,
dreaming of the blue-green waters of the Atlantic
where I watched the porpoises skim the waterline
like living, breathing stones
as I laughed and lit a cigarette,
hearing shouts and lamentations in the distance,
looking up at stars and feeling that
my real home was a planet
with a red sun and yellow mountains
where the voices that woke you came from inside.
And I was dreaming I was a ghost who'd come back

to haunt the ones I love,
sending chills down their spines
at the moment they turn around
to see that no one's there.

I'll be somewhere and someone else tomorrow
or I may be no one and nowhere
but there will be daisies and roses
and big black cars
and people caught in a warm rain
that falls gently on the grass,
on the street,
in all the cities of the world,
on all the planets of the living,
and in the universe of the dead.

Power Lunch

Feeling heavy pressure
from all sides
I bit into
a steak sandwich
and grabbed a handful
of greasy French fries.
As women walked by
in their short skirts
followed by men in
rolled up shirtsleeves,
I realized that
the control I have
over my sandwich
is, for me,
a beautiful and
awesome power.

After the Party

Drunk at four in the morning
my friend Eddie and I
are sitting in this woman's apartment
watching a Depeche Mode video.
On the floor in front of the TV,
some guy she knows
is passed out and snoring
while she sits on the sofa
telling us we should pay attention
to the lyrics being lip-synched
by a skinny English guy
with a fancy haircut
and a fat bank account.
We're both mad
about this woman
but when the song,
the passed-out drunk,
and a night that never ends
seem to surround us
like bad bartenders
serving cheap bourbon
we head out the door saying,
"See you later" "OK,"
and "Bye."

We walk down to the 7-11
and buy some cigarettes,

some bread, and two packages
of canned meatballs with gravy.
We go back to his place,
throw the meatballs with gravy
into a pan, add some cheese,
some leftover spaghetti,
some soy sauce,
and, after a moment's thought,
throw the bread in the pan as well.
We're starting to sober up now
but we're hungry
and this weird mix is, after all,
food of some sort.

Later, after finishing
every last bit of it,
we're sitting at the table
saying nothing.
We're both starting to
feel sick and depressed.
I pour a glass of water
and light a cigarette
as Eddie stares
at his empty plate.

Suddenly Eddie stands up,
walks over to the trash can,

and pukes for a full minute
or two.
When he's done
I walk over to the refrigerator
and grab two cans of beer.
I crack them open and
set one down in front of Eddie.
He looks up at me,
wipes his mouth
with the back of his hand,
and with the light of dawn
coming in through the window
he says, "Shit, man,
it's a brand-new day."

So, we have a toast:
to canned meatballs with gravy,
to all-night parties,
to amateur drunks,
to England and its fancy haircuts,
to all the pretty women in the world,
and to the sun,
which rises high in the sky
over us all.

On the Far Edge of the European Theater

It's animal torture hour
on the Disney channel
at Mike and Mary's house.
Dogs are strung up in trees,
rabbits slit open from head to toe
and cats tossed into the whitewater rapids
as a bearded Frenchman in khaki shorts
sings his country's national anthem.

We're drinking beer and wine,
eating noodles, and playing this card game
called Mille Bornes. We start to speak
French. I cross my eyes and put my hand
inside my shirt. Mike and Mary's
elder son, still just a baby, walks around
the dining room with his finger
in his ass shouting,
"I have a hole, I have a hole."

Outside, the snow has been falling
heavily for five hours now.
If I were to look out the window
I wouldn't be able to see the stars,
but it's all right. Their light
has taken a thousand years to reach me.
I don't mind waiting another day or so.
I know it won't be long

before the clouds roll off
and the bright, blue sky shines
on me, the champion of the march,
great mind of the military,
king of the world.

Night of the Living Dead

There are junkies and homeless people
in my neighborhood,
30-year old men and women
who look twice their age,
50-year old men and women
who no longer look human.
I've seen them throwing down
their change in a Chinese carry-out
or digging up garbage cans
when they didn't even have one penny.
I've heard them talking to themselves,
wandering the streets out of control
or out of touch,
all out of their minds.
They look like they're
out of some horror movie
where the dead come back to life
with an appetite for living human flesh.
Perhaps one day they'll
stop going to cheap carry-outs.
They'll walk right by the garbage cans
and head straight
for the guy wearing the three-piece suit.
Instead of asking him for change
they'll just roll up his sleeve
and take a bite out of his arm,
pull down his trousers

and tear a chunkful of fatty flesh
from his ass.
They'll eat everyone: bank tellers,
architects, football heroes, centerfold models.
They'll eat the nuns and priests
and the guy who runs the soup kitchen too.
Then, when they've eaten all
the so-called living people,
they'll eat each other,
killing each other off.
And when the last of them dies
all the cows and chickens
and lambs and pigs will roam
the streets and the sun will shine
and the cows will chase the chickens
and the pigs will chase the cows
and the lambs will just lie there,
on bloodstained streets,
waiting to inherit the earth.

The Sporting Life

I think I have a future
in baseball
playing third base
on a team
with better-than-average hitting
and a stadium on
the outskirts of town.
I feel I have
a chance at cornerback
on a football team
that emphasizes defense
and speed
and has cheerleaders
who wear red striped skirts
and black underwear.
I believe I can
get a spot
on a basketball team
that needs a point guard
with a sore left heel
and a tendency
to get drunk
before the game.
I understand that
in hockey the goalie
doesn't need great skating ability
so much as the skill
to handle the things

that take him by surprise.
I've learned that
the best thing about
golf is that it's not
a team sport and
if you feel like quitting
you just put your ball
in your pocket
and leave.

And I know
that when I have to run,
I can:

on the track
on the street
or to the other side
of the room,
where there's a door
I can open as I say,
"Goodbye, I'm
not going to
see you anymore.
You'll have to
play this game
without me."

Deep End

Last night it occurred to me
that I might be losing my mind.
What else could drive me
to watch my health,
go on a diet,
eat salads for dinner,
quit smoking,
quit drinking,
exercise for an hour a day
and fall in love with a nice girl.

But today I've just eaten
a big greasy bacon cheeseburger,
opened my third pack
of cigarettes for the day
and downed my sixth bourbon
in two hours.
I'm staring at this plump woman
who's wearing a halter top
and about a pound of mascara
around her bloodshot eyes.

When the room begins to spin
I smile, comforted.

September Song

When I was a kid in grade school
the teacher once made us repeat after her,
"The key to success is hard work."
Years later, in college, another teacher told us,
"You have to work hard to get an A
and you have to work hard to get an F."
One thing they never told you
was that sometimes you could make it
without any effort at all.
This you had to learn on your own.
And though it's true
that most of the time
you have to slave away
to get anywhere,
the most beautiful moments
are those when you find yourself
in the right place at the right time,
or when, after doing something easy,
you find yourself suddenly
on top of the mountain.

Sometimes when you're at the racetrack
and you forget about the jockey,
the odds and past performance
and bet big on a horse
because you like its name,
you go home with a hundred dollars

you didn't have that morning.
Sometimes, wandering the streets aimlessly,
looking for nothing,
just walking like a zombie,
you run into a friend
and end up drinking and laughing,
ready once again to look
at the world that surrounds you.

This is the beauty of the moment
that comes alive without artifice,
the beauty of the mountain
that is built without industry
without business,

without blueprints and guidelines
and a right way
and a wrong way.

It's the beauty of being human,
of not always making sense,
the beauty of falling and getting up
not because there are things to do,
but simply because you have fallen
too deeply into the realm of the possible,
and it's time to do
what you were told

you couldn't do,
and you do it effortlessly
and easily high
and wide
and running, on these
still golden days.

The Big One

My bonds to failure are stronger
than my bonds to triumph.
But I promise not to tell this
if you promise not to listen
when I break all my past commitments
and finally win the big one.

III.

Original Love

Chivalry

Empty days when it's tough
just to face a bowl of Jell-O
in the morning. When the wind
blowing on a tree's bare thin branches
reminds you of
your rattled nerves.
Days when you're jealous
of the dogs fucking in the backyard,
days when you want to scream
at people wearing three-piece suits
who spend their lunch hours
banging away at pin ball machines
when you're trying to drink
your beer in peace.
Days when the entire atmosphere
seems to bear down on you
like a gigantic bird of prey
ready to drop a load.
Days like that I think even Jesus
would look at me sideways,
Buddha would tell me
to turn to hard drugs
and Mohammed would advise me
to eat more pork

as he smiles and pulls out
a stainless-steel scimitar.

And so tonight, when a woman
I've been trying to impress
with my appreciation
of art and poetry
sees me stumble out
of a strip tease joint, drunk,
clutching a dancer's blue lace panties,
I come to think
that there are other things
more important to me
than blue lace panties,
and so I toss them
to the sidewalk
and wave to her
as I try to remember
just what those things are.

My Own Like Poem

Leslie,
I like you.
I don't think you're
a jerk like
Michael does
why I even like
the way you eat
strawberries.

You interrupt the silence
the way Tahiti
interrupts the ocean.

Don't change.

I'm going away for now.
I'll be back soon.

Bye bye.

Bye.

I Can't Find My Money

Ever since I threw up
in the hole
of my guitar,
my guitar playing
hasn't been
the same.
Now when I
stand beneath
my true love's
window
to serenade her,
she no longer
blows me a kiss
and throws me
her key,
but calls
the cops
instead.

Oh, love,
oh, love.

What am I
doing wrong?

Fall Blues

Wednesday's painted red,
all the thrill gone out of strumming,
waiting tremulously on a number
my last two dollars disappear.

I stand half drunk in the middle
of the street, arms akimbo,
wishing I had a car and someone else's
credit card. I could leave all this

behind. Different rooms, beds, and chairs
every night, fresh towels every morning,
living lazily, life dropped down
from a redwood or some cloud
I don't know the name of.
It could be like sleeping.

81 St. Mark's Place

Ice cream
in noisy glass
cups:
the TV's on
in the dark
and the phone
and doorbell keep
ringing.
We're
watching
cartoons.

Work

It's the exceedingly normal
situation that distresses me most —
watching television and laughing
at the jokes Jay Leno
tells his Friday night audience;
wives and children on a Saturday morning,
the smell of grass, the sound
of a lawnmower in the air;
on Sunday driving to church,
relaxing by the pool
and going to bed early
to be ready for work the next day.

If we start to love
let's not just live together
and let's not work.
We'll go out where
the grass grows tall
and the water tastes of salt,
where a moment of leisure
is as natural as the glow
of moonlight on skin.
And even though our babies
will be born, we'll try to keep
the children inside us.

End of the Parade

I feel a sense of wonder
in the heat of this kaleidoscope summer.
The show is on again in the streets,
and the sight of a sexy woman
in a tight leather miniskirt
strolling by with her man who's in a tee-shirt
with the sleeves rolled up
to show off his perfect muscles
makes you believe
that evolution is working.
People probably look better now
than they did two thousand years ago.
They can run faster, jump higher,
eat better, and live longer.
It's a new and improved society
of Greek gods and goddesses,
where people are being
all they can be,
finding a better life through
aerobics, psychotherapy,
financial planning,
and macrobiotic cooking,
while dressed in
what I think are
Bugle Boy Jeans,
but I'm not about to ask.

Somehow, when I close my eyes,
what I see is so much better.
A woman, a little older, her body beaten down
somewhat by strange weather
and words, touching me with a
gentle tap on the shoulder
and saying,
"Let's go home now.
We've seen
enough."

Original Love

Original love was a sentimental love song which when
played backwards said "Satan is my friend forever,

motherfucker." The big bang was when Adam got Eve
pregnant with Cain or Abel or whichever of those good

or bad young men was their first son. As for me, the first
song I ever sang didn't get me a girlfriend, didn't make

my best friend in high school's girlfriend leave my best
friend, who was kind of a dick. My first woman had nothing

to do with the art of song, and even less involvement with
anything one might call love. There was work and money,

long evenings spent in bars, and train rides like morning
headaches, vacations at the beach, cross country trips on the

bus or on the plane and people who were either impressed
or appalled that I had a job, a car, and a foreign sounding name.

After that came no work, and no money, occasional run ins
with the great but more often with the not-so-great, and

phone calls from bill collectors who threatened to sue me,
and death threats from people who were once my friends.

True love came later when I had nothing and knew nothing.
It took me by surprise at a time when all I expected was

a steady downpour of noise and scorn and rain. And though
the great flood may be yet to come, and the big bang a myth

that never happened, I remember that in the beginning I had
a dream where bees hovered around me as if I were a clear jar

of raw brown honey, flew about my arms and legs and face
as I stood on a high wire in the open air above the street with

all its cars and buses and people with their skyward gazes
and breathless whispers. And I remember one nearly perfect

evening when my spirit turned around and around like a planet
spinning and circling around all the days and years which

I thought would never come, the original love that kept
the bees from stinging and the jar shut tight. And I remember

it was original love that brought me to this moment, moved me
from school and work and money to here, to this tightrope

on which I walk, knowing that whether or not I make it to
the other side I will fall—deeply and completely, with

a gesture of tremendous force and grace, and like a man
who, despite his many failings, remains great for all time.

IV.

Fuckups of the Lower East Side

A True Star

My friend Michael and I
are sitting at an outdoor cafe
on Avenue A, drinking beer,
when we spot Lady Miss Kier,
the singer of the hot new band
Deee-Lite.
She's walking down the street
dressed in a psychedelic body suit
which she fills
like the "m" in
$e=mc^2$.
Everyone at the cafe,
everyone on the street,
and everyone in the windows
of the buildings on Avenue A
stops eating, drinking, driving,
to watch Lady Miss Kier
as she goes by,
and my friend Michael says,
"Now there's a true star."

And with those words I start to wish
that I had the sort of talent
and presence that could get me
fame and admiration,
but the only talents I have
are for drinking beer

and fucking up.
Very common talents, yes,
but I'm working on
doing them with great style
and in great proportions,
so that one day,
when I walk down Avenue A
to buy beer at the store,
people will stop and say,
"Hey, that guy's
the biggest drunk in town."
People will stop their cars
in the middle of the street,
walk up to me and say,

"You're the guy who came to town
and fucked up REALLY big. . . .
Can I have your autograph?"
"Sure," I'll say,
and I'll sign their copies of
Fuckups of the Lower East Side
with the words,
"From a great fuckup
to a little fuckup.
Here's looking
down
at you."

Land of the Giants, 1996

Manute Bol hovers by the bar when we can't find the money—
he's eight feet tall and we've overstayed our welcome.
We walk out of there thinking there's nothing wrong,
leaving the car keys on the table along with our empties.
And then we find the money.

At another bar the Channel Four reporter shoves me out of the way
and we follow him out the door, then give up and catch a cab
like secret agents whose assignment has just been cancelled
or two witnesses leaving the scene of a crime
neither of us will report.

We've seen worse, done worse, have answered
the call of the wild wearing bad sneakers and bad hats.
When it's cold nobody knows your name
and even old friends call you "sir" or "madam."

Twenty years ago "Convoy" was the number one song in the country.
Ten years ago the space shuttle Challenger blew up
without ever reaching orbit.
Five years ago, the lambada dance craze fizzled.

But today the snow is melting
and tiny ice floes float on the river
and people are "out and about" and "on the mend"
and "ready to make a comeback."
Or so they say.

It's like that sometimes. You're like that sometimes.
I'm like this.

For the Saints and Angels, Miles Davis, and You

Miles Davis was a skinny motherfucker, a bitter and often mean man.
I have always been a little on the stocky side and while often bitter,
       I am rarely mean.

Miles Davis was a master trumpet player while the only thing I've mastered
is the art of keeping my better qualities concealed like money
       people hide in their shoes.

Miles Davis was a performer who most of the time would have
       preferred to just rip your eyes out rather than accept
       your applause.
I am a performer who most of the time would prefer to just rip your
       eyes out rather than accept your applause.

Whenever Miles Davis wanted to make money he'd just pick up his horn,
play it, and come home with several thousand dollars.
Whenever I want to make money I write a story and two months later
       I get a check in the mail for a hundred and fifty bucks or less.
       (Usually less.)

During the course of his life Miles Davis went to Paris, Tokyo, London.
The longest trip I ever made was the time I took a Greyhound from
       New Orleans to Las Vegas with a stomach flu.

Miles Davis—people always seem to obsess over him.
Like the Irish Catholic girl I knew in college who said,
       "All I know about jazz is Miles Davis."

Like the kid watching a man play trumpet
        on the corner of St. Mark's Place and Avenue A
and saying to him,
        "Hey, man, play some Miles Davis."

As far as I know no one has ever obsessed over me,
        and though I have heard stories of people other than me
reciting my poems in public
        I believe these reports to be greatly exaggerated.

I remember when Miles Davis died.
I was at a girlfriend's apartment in New York
        and they'd been playing Miles Davis on WKCR all weekend.

We'd gone out for Chinese food and when we got back
to her place she suddenly turned catatonic,
giving me an evil look as *Sketches of Spain*
        came out of the radio.

"What's wrong?" I asked, "Was it something I said?"
She just sat there on her living room chair saying nothing,
and after a while I walked out the door,
        went home and turned on the TV.

Miles Davis would have screamed
"What the fuck's wrong with you, bitch?"
        before picking up the phone to call one of his other girls.

"Mary," he'd say, or "Martha" or "Johanna" or any of a hundred other names,
"This is Miles. Meet me at the corner of Second Avenue and Eleventh Street
in ten minutes, and make sure you're wearing that red silk dress I gave you."
Click.

Miles Davis is dead,
though I, at the moment, am alive
            and remembering the night, two years after he died,
when, contemplating the wind's direction, I stood
on the corner of Broadway and West 57th Street
            in a crucifixion pose.

Elsewhere the Eiffel Tower was standing tall and Big Ben still
            ringing as the lights of Tokyo pushed out the darkness.
And with the November cold sliding through my winter coat,
            I put my arms back down and walked
like on a Sunday morning in the spring
            when the blood rushes through your veins,
only it wasn't spring and it wasn't Sunday,
            and I wasn't anywhere near heaven
with no money in my pocket, no tune to play
            and no made-up angel in a silk dress
            to take me home.

Miles Davis
is long gone and so is

Jesus, Buddha, Muhammad or whosoever
        has inspired or moved you
but at least you
        are still alive.

So let your idols expire. Let there be joy
on Broad Street and bedlam uptown.
        Let young hearts and your own be crushed.

Commerce will work against you once again,
        but the law of the land
        is a wasp with mud on its wings
and honey in its left eye.
        Its belly is full
but its heart is a sponge:
        kill it before it kills you because
the gods will never punish you,
        and the saints and angels will never squeal on you,
only men whose names have
        already been forgotten. . . .

The Angel of 11th Street

At the end of another drunken week
of beer and whiskey and wine
I walked home
and on the street I met a woman
who bummed a cigarette from me
and offered a piece of candy in return.
She told me she was heading
to 11th Street by St. Mark's Church
to make money giving guys blow jobs.
She was young and beautiful and spoke
in tones of the brightest white light,
and I wished her luck, said goodbye
and walked away.

And I've seen people hit by cars
and people ODing on the street
as crowds gathered to watch,
and I've seen people staring
into space at nothing
because there was nothing left to see
that didn't make them sad or mad or weary,
and I've seen men and women
step from the doorways of buildings
where their friends or lovers live,
each parting a necessary loss
when the only thing left to be
is alone.

And as the days go by
what I remember most
is the distance between things,
the endings of great moments and pleasures,
and as you walk
in the sharp eye of the midday sun
or beneath the cum-colored shining
of a crescent moon
the weather is always
the same.

And tonight
the Angel of 11th Street
is standing on a corner
selling blow jobs and buying candy
to keep the devil at arm's length
and heaven close to the steady beating
of her untainted heart.

On Broadway

In a hotel bar
on 47th and Broadway,
there's bourbon and pretzels on the table,
a copy of my hometown paper by the window,
and I'm chatting with the waitress,
an old girlfriend of mine.
On the TV is a baseball game—
it's the Twins vs. the Blue Jays,
and though I've had several hours worth
of strong drinks and stale cigarettes
I'm not seeing two of anything
and the only birds I see are
in my mind.

At the end of the night
I get into a cab with the waitress,
and as we head downtown
in the after-midnight noise and lights,
Times Square suddenly becomes
Amsterdam, Bangkok, Berlin,
and I feel like we're tourists on holiday
taking each passing minute
on the cuff.

But I'm thinking
that maybe this is really Disneyland,
and we're children,

feeling what we're supposed to feel
as we hold our tickets in hand
waiting to go on a ride through the heart
of a shrinking world
that will abandon us
as love and magic had long ago.

The New York City Marathon

Some people say they rarely
ever go above 14th Street.
Others say they won't bother
with anything going on above Houston.

As for me, there are days
when I never get out of bed,
which means, I guess,
THAT I WIN.

Angel

I am an angel. I live in outer space but you call it
heaven. I sit immobile but you think I have wings.
Though I watch your every move, I have no stake
in your health or happiness. Though I manifest
my being in every moment of your lives, my actions
are petty and trivial. When you walk through the park
on the first warm day of spring, I'm the force
that makes the pigeon shit on your head.
When you sit in a stall in a public restroom
I'm the power that makes the toilet paper disappear
the moment you're ready to wipe.
I'm the desire that drives the cute little five-year-old
to give you the finger when you smile at him.
I am the knowledge that no matter what line
you pick at the supermarket, it will be the slowest.

I am the reason Celine Dion is a huge star, the reason
your penis is two inches long, the reason your breasts
are as flat as the Great Plains. I am the bitter aftertaste
in sugar substitutes; your morning hangover. I am dandruff,
an ingrown toenail, a speck of dust in your eye, a pebble
in your comfortable new shoes. I am the fitful sleep in which
you dream and find yourself falling from a mountain.
I am the revelation in which you discover that you are
neither great nor original but empty-headed and common.

As for those greater catastrophes, those fatal accidents,
those terminal diseases, poverty, war, and famine, I stake

no claim. I compose neither good nor evil, justice nor injustice,
but convenience and inconvenience. All my works are shallow and trite.

I am merely an attendant, serving the way I was meant to serve,
following the orders of a monarch who devotes his time to greater things.
And when sirens echo in the distance I do not hear them.
When rivers overflow I do not see them washing away your cities.

In the beginning was the darkness, then came the light.
Though I am of that light I do not help you see.
And as you walk through your world blind, I give you
no hint of what's to come, no sign telling you to go or to stop—
just an aching in your bones, the self-conscious knowledge
that somewhere, in the middle of this universe,
away from the greatness of kings, you exist.

Why I'm So Much Greater Than Everyone Else

My peerless intelligence
and keen wit.
My good looks and vast
                physical prowess.
Above all, my sensitivity to
your needs—most importantly
your need to serve and praise me.

I am the outer limit,
the stuff dreams are made of,
the unmoved mover
who sets the wheels in motion,
the big cigar of perpetual smoking.

I hold my head so high
                I get nose bleeds.

A Short History of Everyone in the World

On the train going
back to my hometown
people are laughing at the
drunk who's making fun
of the bald spot on a guy
a few rows up.
Across the aisle from me
a deaf man is making garbled passes
at all the women walking by
on the way to the club car.
Next to me a girl
with a silly haircut
is drinking a beer and
talking to everyone in sight
between drags of her cigarette.
It's one of those
holiday weekend party trains
where everyone's celebrating
and ready to tell their life story.

The drunk guy is going
to Richmond where he'll find a bar
and drink some more.
The haircut girl is going
to Philadelphia—she plans
to become a hairdresser.
The guy with the bald spot
has just gotten out of prison—

he's trying to stay
calm and out of trouble.
The deaf guy is just horny
and doesn't bother to read
the lips of the women
who tell him to fuck off.

When the haircut girl
asks me for my story
I tell her,
"I saved up my money
to buy this train ticket
so I could visit home

and get there comfortably.
I cut my spending in half
by eating my own shit.
Why I've been living off
the same macaroni and cheese
dinner for two months now."

"Oh," she says, startled, grimacing.

"Excuse me," I say. "I have
to go to the bathroom now."

When I stand up,
everyone's quiet,

and I know that when
I get back to my seat
I'll be able to just relax
and sleep.
No stories, no loud laughter,
no more rude comments,
snide remarks or subtle innuendoes.
I'd put an end to that
because I'd just said all
there was in the world
to be said.

The Complete Failure of Everything

At the carnival sideshow
the veteran sword swallower has bloodied his throat.
The snake charmer has been attacked—
his cobras, rattlers, boas
have stung, bitten, and squeezed him to death.
In the tunnel of love the teenage couple
keep their hands at their sides and
look straight ahead,
waiting anxiously for the ride to end.
Out on the rollercoaster people are yawning
while on the merry-go-round children
are screaming in terror.
In the suburbs a man has decided
not to build a deck on the back
of his new house.
His neighbors are at the mall
attending the grand opening
of a multiplex porno theater.
Back in town the crack dealers
and junkie hookers
are preaching the word of the lord.
The Jehovah's Witnesses are wandering around
drunk, cigarettes dangling from their mouths
as they mumble, "Jesus, I just don't know."
In the universities the professors
have taken over the libraries.
They're tearing up the pages

of every book on every shelf
on every subject.
In the nightclub the stripper
with the 72-inch bust is keeping her top on
while the flat-chested women
rip open their blouses
and shout, "Va Va Voom,"
to the delight
of the already frenzied crowd.
The billionaire is sitting on a park bench
perusing the want ads
while the panhandler orders dinner
at a fancy French restaurant
for fifty of his closest friends.

There is snow in the desert
and flowers in the arctic,
wild music in the asylums
and silence in the dance halls,
charity in the casinos
and greed at the Salvation Army,
orgies in the convents
and prayer in the whorehouses.

And what we are witnessing
is the complete failure of everything.

The failure of the rich and the poor,
the failure of the ecstatic and the tortured,
the failure of the loud and the peaceful,
the failure of love and hate,
the beautiful and the ugly,
the good and the bad,
the daring and the timid.

It's the failure of the holy to stay holy
and the sinners to keep sinning,
the failure of the rich to stay rich
and the poor to stay poor,
the failure of those who love to love,
and those who hate to hate,
everything failing right to the end,
where the big bang,
having reached its limit,
reverses itself,
with everything you know
falling apart,
here, in the carnival
where the last great act
is to take something,

and through a swift sleight of hand
turn it into nothing

as the bright lights dim
and the merry-go-round
grinds slowly
to a complete
and silent
stop.

On These Days Driving

Perfection is all those horrible old love affairs
they tell their latest lover about in bed as they smoke
cigarettes, together and laughing in the darkness.
Perfection is all those bad years spent starving,
mad, aimless, before finally finding a way, through
chance or struggle, to make it.
Perfection is the moment when the worst
is behind you and the best slowly reveals itself
like a song from decades ago that only now
becomes a hit.

I confess that I've got it all
ass-backwards, that perfection is beyond me
and my best was long ago,
with the worst now revealing itself
like the dream you can't remember,
the dream that leaves you gasping for air
as you sit up,
scared and alone,
staring out into the infinite darkness.

I never liked perfection,
I never tried to make the pieces
fit neatly, cleanly, exactly.

I always like the team that worked
the hardest, yet blew it in the end
and came in second,

the movie star who grew old and crazy,
forgot her lines and faded away . . .
it was something about the blemish on her cheek,
the hint of insanity,
the look on the players' faces,
which whether out of lame stupidity
or brave wisdom, seemed to say
that things just weren't right.

And though there hasn't been
a day in the last twenty or so years
when I haven't at least
considered the possibilities

of jumping out a fifth-floor window
or throwing myself into the middle
of rush hour traffic
on the interstate,

I don't.

So, if you see me
in the late evening
or early morning
walking the streets, looking up
for shadows in the facades of buildings,
or on the road driving past

The International House of Pancakes,
The Food Lion, and The Best Western
by the airport,
ready to swerve,
just keep in mind that as far as I know
I'm on the right highway,
and moving in the right direction,
with the grey and white signs
leading me westward
into the deep, imperfect blue.

NOTES

"A True Star" is for Michael Randall
"Avenue Banana" is for Gail Schilke
"Land of the Giants" is for Ceridwen Morris
"My First Poem" is for Leah Hofkin
"Strange Dreams" is for Carl Watson